Everyday Prayers for Nurses

EVERYDAY
PRAYERS
for
Nurses

Barry Culbertson
and
Penny Vaughn

DIMENSIONS
FOR LIVING
NASHVILLE

EVERYDAY PRAYERS FOR NURSES
Barry Culbertson and Penny Vaughn

Copyright © 1996 by Dimensions for Living

96 97 98 99 00 01 02 03 04 05 — 10 9 8 7 6 5 4 3 2 1

This book is printed on acid-free recycled paper.
ISBN 0-687-18423-1

MANUFACTURED IN THE UNITED STATES OF AMERICA

Contents

For Change in the Hospital 10

For Change in Health Care 11

To Be in Your Service 12

Why, Lord? 13

The Miracle of Life 14

For Those Who Make Decisions 15

For an Addicted Friend 16

Caring for an Abused Child 17

For an Elderly Patient 18

For an Addicted Patient 19

For My Family 20

For Our Bodies 21

For Not Being Judgmental 22

Should I Seek Further Education? 23

My Friend Has Cancer 24

My First Day of Work   25

For New Nurses   26

For My Students   27

For Home Care   28

The Gift of Teaching   29

Home Visits   30

For the Parents of a Stillborn Baby   31

For Parents Expecting a Baby
   with Birth Defects   32

For Empty Lives   33

Dealing with a Heavy Workload   34

Letting a Patient Go   35

For the Loss of a Loved One   36

On the Birth of a Baby   37

For an Unmarried Mother   38

For a Patient Addicted to Alcohol   39

For One Who Is Terminally Ill   40

For a Lonely Patient   41

For the Parents of a Chronically
   Sick Child   42

For an Abused Child Going Home   43
For a Dying Patient   44
To Be a Witness   45
For a Responsible Teenager   46
Working in a Community Hospital   47
Making Administrative Decisions   48
For Teaching Skills   49
For Helping a Lonely Patient   50
To Be an Advocate   51
I Lost a Patient   52
Thank You for My Work   53
I Made a Mistake   54
On a Snowy Day   55
For My Staff   56
For Understanding in a Disaster   57
For Making a Career Decision   58
For Working with the Dying   59
Starting an I. V.   60
For Healing from Medications   61
Waiting for the Ambulance   62

For Guidance   63
For the Ending of the Day   64
On Fixing Lunch   65
For Physicians   66
For the Health Team   67
Before a Staff Meeting   68
My Role in a Staff Meeting   69
On Changing Shifts   70
When Charting   71
For a Patient Going to Surgery   72
For Those Who Wait   73
Before Performing a Painful Procedure   74
For a Severely Depressed Patient   75
For a Demanding Patient   76
At a Birth   77
For Bearing Witness   78
Laughter   79
A Prayer During Quiet Time in
   the Chapel   80
Prayer on the Way to Work   81

At the End of a Shift   82

For the Physician   83

As a "Stat/Code Blue" Begins   84

Prayer Over Medications   85

Waiting for a New Patient   86

After a Misunderstanding   87

Witnessing to One of Another Faith   88

For a Patient Who Has Received
   Bad News   89

To Serve in Your Name   90

A Prayer for a New Employee   91

For the Lonely   92

For One Whose Life Is Forever
   Changed   93

To Bring Comfort   94

Let Me Rest in You   95

For Your Constant Love and Care   96

For Change in the Hospital

Dear Lord, there is so much change taking place in my hospital. Help me to be an agent of positive outcomes, and lead me away from negative conversations and attitudes. As changes evolve, help us all to remain focused on our patients. AMEN.

For Change in Health Care

God of grace, there is so much change taking place in health care. Change frightens me. I fear that patient care will suffer. Lord, I pray that decisions made for me and my patients will be honest and just and will bring about an improved health care system. AMEN.

To Be in Your Service

Dear Lord, today is a new opportunity for me to be in service in your name. Give me wisdom and compassion as I provide care for my patients. AMEN.

Why, Lord?

Our Father, I am feeling the need to know why. Fill me with your assurance and comfort so that I can minister to my patients and their families when tragedy strikes. AMEN.

The Miracle of Life

God of the living, I praise your name as
I reflect on the miracle of life, on the
marvelous, intricate design and function of
the human body. Thank you for allowing
me to be a part of your healing ministry.
AMEN.

For Those Who Make Decisions

O God our guide, change in health care is causing me and my co-workers to feel insecure and frustrated. I pray for those in our government and hospital administration who are making decisions about health care delivery. May their decisions be right and just. AMEN.

For an Addicted Friend

My God, my friend at work is dealing with drug addiction. I know it, Lord. How do I help? Give me the insight and direction I need to help my friend, AMEN.

Caring for an Abused Child

Lord of compassion, I come to you with a great deal of anger. How can parents abuse a child? Guide my actions and attitudes as I care for this child and interact with the parents. AMEN.

For an Elderly Patient

My Lord, Miss Sally is better today. Thank you for the healing that has taken place in her elderly body. Dear Lord, she has no place to go, no one to help her. Father, direct me in finding her the assistance she needs. AMEN.

For an Addicted Patient

Precious Savior, help me to share your saving grace with my patient who is addicted to drugs. Help me to assist him in knowing that he is your special creation, that he is valuable in your eyes. Replace his craving for drugs with a hunger and thirst for knowing you. AMEN.

For My Family

Dear Father, my family is so precious to me. Thank you for blessing me with a spouse and children. As I leave my work with my patients and enter my home, give me energy and patience to take care of my family. AMEN.

For Our Bodies

Dear Lord, what a marvelous creation you have made in the human body. I praise your name as I witness the function of the body in both health and illness. Thank you for making our physical bodies capable of healing. Thank you for allowing me to be a part of this healing ministry. AMEN.

For Not Being Judgmental

Dear Lord of righteousness and justice, I know the Scriptures warn me of the consequences of judging. But Lord, I'm having a difficult time not judging my patient. It appears that she has chosen a lifestyle and habits that have brought about this deadly illness. She will die. I don't want to be involved. I feel hopeless, helpless, and angry. Oh Lord, forgive me, forgive me. Fill me with your peace and allow me to pass on your unconditional love to my patient. AMEN.

Should I Seek Further Education?

Dear Father, I chose to be a nurse because I wanted to help the sick get well and whole. I feel the need to continue my education so that I can be a better nurse. I pray for your guidance in this decision. Lord, lead me to the right place of higher education. Help me to find the financial assistance I need. Allow me to feel the comfort of your presence, so that I know I am making the right decision. AMEN.

My Friend Has Cancer

Our healing Lord, I learned today that my friend, who is also a nurse, has cancer. I am devastated for her and for her family. Her children are small, and her husband depends on her for so much. I pray that the miraculous drugs and therapies that we administer every day will heal my friend. AMEN.

My First Day of Work

Dear God, this is my first day of work since graduating from school. I feel so incapable of performing these tasks safely and competently. The experienced nurses seem so organized and confident. Help me to learn from them. Be with me, Lord, on this first day of my professional dream! Amen.

For New Nurses

Dear Father, as these new nurses come to us today, I see terror in their eyes. Help us to be positive role models for them. Give us kindness and patience in dealing with their questions and insecurities. Assist us in guiding their actions so that they will become competent, caring nurses. AMEN.

For My Students

Our Lord, my students are preparing to take final examinations. I pray that I have taught them well. I pray for their success in completing these evaluations. AMEN.

For Home Care

Dear heavenly Father, as I enter my patient's home today, assist me in being accurate in my assessment. I know that I am the only health professional that my patient will see today. Help me to be perceptive of her needs. AMEN.

The Gift of Teaching

My God, I praise your name and thank you for giving me the gift of teaching. As I prepare to assist my patients in understanding their illnesses and their treatments, guide my words and actions. Help me to minister to all of their needs while they are in my class. AMEN.

Home Visits

Dear Father, thank you for this opportunity to visit my patients in their homes. These home visits allow me to know about their total environment. Help me to be perceptive of their needs. Enable me to find the assistance they need. Some of their situations seem so impossible, but Lord, I know you will guide me as I seek resources and treatments for my patients. AMEN.

For the Parents of a Stillborn Baby

Dear comforting Father, as I listened to my patient's physician give her the bad news, my heart broke for her. Her baby did not survive birth. She and her husband are devastated. Help me to be a source of comfort and strength to them in your name. AMEN.

For Parents Expecting a Baby with Birth Defects

Loving Lord, my patient and her husband have learned that their baby is likely to be born with birth defects. They have chosen to have the baby instead of terminating the pregnancy. I admire their courage and faith. Help me to be a source of strength and support to them. AMEN.

For Empty Lives

My Savior, some of my co-workers are struggling with life. They feel an empty space in their lives. I know the answer to filling their emptiness and restlessness. Enable me, through the Holy Spirit, to effectively witness to them about you, my Savior. AMEN.

Dealing with a Heavy Workload

My Sustainer: What a day! I have so many patients for whom to provide care. I can't keep up this pace and effectively take care of my patients. Help me to find solutions to this workload, so that my co-workers and I can provide competent care for our patients. AMEN.

Letting a Patient Go

O living Lord, I have watched my
patient hold on to life through this
complex, painful therapy. It appears that,
while he has fought the good fight, he
cannot survive his illness. I don't want to
let him go. I don't want to give up. Lord,
allow me to give him up to a more glorious
life in you. Give him the peace that only
you can give. AMEN.

For the Loss of a Loved One

My Lord, the Good Shepherd, be with this family as they experience the loss of life of their loved one. They have been so faithful in their prayers. They have remained attentive to their loved one and to each other. Thank you for giving them this time to say "good-bye." Allow them to feel your loving arms of comfort and peace. AMEN.

On the Birth of a Baby

Lord, our Maker, thank you for the gift of new life. What a beautiful sight! Uphold and sustain these new parents as they take this precious new life home. Give them wisdom and patience. May they live a life patterned on Jesus Christ as they guide and nurture this blessed child. AMEN.

For an Unmarried Mother

God of hope, the birth of a baby should be such a happy time. But Lord, this young, unmarried mother has a life of struggle ahead of her. I pray that you will assist her in finding employment, child care, and a husband who will love her and her child. Give her wisdom beyond her years to love and care for this child. AMEN.

For a Patient Addicted to Alcohol

My God who provides, no matter how much faith I have, some situations seem so impossible. What are we going to do with this patient? This is his third visit to our Emergency Department this week. He drinks so much that he is sick and poorly nourished all of the time. Help us to treat him with respect as part of your creation. Help us to find resources to save him. AMEN.

For One Who Is Terminally Ill

My Refuge in times of trouble, we have worked so hard to keep this patient alive. Now it is the time to decide whether to continue care or terminate our efforts. This decision always makes me feel so uncomfortable, as if we were "playing God." Lord, give us the wisdom and compassion we need to assist the family in making this decision. I pray that our decision will not be based on expense of care or lack of faith. Father, may our decision be in your will. AMEN.

For a Lonely Patient

My God, my guide, this home visit is trying my patience! I know that my patient is lonely. I know that her stubbornness and refusal to comply with her treatment are her ways of getting my attention. Give me patience to meet her needs, to listen to her with caring and concern. Thank you, Father, for giving me this ministry. AMEN.

For the Parents of a Chronically Sick Child

Lord of peace, there is so much tension in this home. These parents are so stressed by their child's illness and their financial situation. Each blames the other. They all feel guilty. They are unable to help and support each other. Their spiritual resources are as low as their financial resources. Help me, Lord, to be a mediator and a source of hope. Help me to find resources to meet both their financial and spiritual needs. AMEN.

For an Abused Child Going Home

God who loves and protects little children, I feel so uncomfortable sending this child back to his home. He looks at me with pleading eyes, eyes that show the fear and powerlessness he feels. I have tried to intervene, without success. The courts have spoken. Lord, protect this child. AMEN.

For a Dying Patient

Father of unconditional love, Mary has so abused her body that she is consumed with disease. She has shared parts of her life with me. My heart breaks for her. She never had a chance. Help me to show her your love in these last moments of her life. Help me to give her hope for a new life in Christ, a life of peace, love, and acceptance. AMEN.

To Be a Witness

Dear Lord of second chances, what an opportunity you gave me today! My patient was really seeking a witness to life in Jesus. I was afraid of being an ineffective witness. I was afraid that I would turn him away from you. I did not trust you to empower me with the right words. Forgive me, Lord! Give me another opportunity to witness for you. AMEN.

For a Responsible Teenager

Dear Jesus, we need to give Bobby so much more than medicine. At sixteen he is the adult in his family. His dad is absent and his mom is a drug addict. He has six younger brothers and sisters. You have given him a conscience to do what is right. He needs now to be in control off his diabetes and to find positive help for his family. Lord, help us to help him in all his needs. AMEN.

Working in a Community Hospital

Dear Lord who provides, I love my community hospital. We try to be good caregivers so that our patients can stay near home. But Lord, you know that our resources are slim. We are struggling to stay in business. Guide us, Lord, to find ways to keep our facility operational for our patients and their families. AMEN.

Making Administrative Decisions

God, my refuge, as Nursing Administrator I have had to make some really tough decisions today. Guide my decisions and actions. Give me the wisdom I need to deal with this business. My main concern is for my nursing staff and our patients. Help me to be an advocate for them all to ensure a place of quality nursing care. Instill in my staff the desire to be their best for their patients. AMEN.

For Teaching Skills

Jesus, the example of teachers, my
nurses have to know so much today to
provide care for seriously ill patients with
complex problems. They are working
harder and doing more with less support
and fewer resources. Help me to teach
them well so that they may return to their
workplaces with confidence, enthusiasm,
and renewed energy. Help them to be a
positive force in their clinical
environments as they provide
knowledgeable, competent care with
compassion. AMEN.

For Helping a Lonely Patient

Jesus, my Redeemer, as I try to complete all my tasks today, I have neglected Mr. Brown. He wants to talk and talk. I know that he is lonely. He has no visitors. Give me time, Lord, to spend meaningful moments with him. I know that my time and attention are sources of healing for him. AMEN.

To Be an Advocate

Dear Father, my refuge in time of disaster, I know that a disaster is about to happen. I know that doctors have more education and training than I do. But I know I am right about this patient. Give me the right words and attitude to be an advocate for my patient. Give the physician wisdom and a sense of humility as he determines this patient's treatment. Help us to be able to work together in harmony for our patient's sake. AMEN.

I Lost a Patient

Dear God of all creation, sometimes life is such a mystery. I feel certain we did all of the right things in treating this patient, but she died anyway. She was so small, so young, so precious. I am feeling the need to know why children die. Give me the peace I need about this situation. Restore my faith. AMEN.

Thank You for My Work

God of grace and glory, if today all I do is give my patients hope, I will praise your name. Thank you for this rewarding work. Thank you for giving me the courage and ability to minister to patients in your name. AMEN.

I Made a Mistake

Dear Lord, my ever present help in time of trouble, I made a mistake today. I know there may be legal consequences to my action. I am terrified, Lord, that my patient might die. Lord, save my patient. Give me courage to practice again, for all I want to do now is run away! AMEN.

On a Snowy Day

Jesus, my light, as I reported to work on this cold, snowy day, all I could think about was the luxury of staying at home, in bed. Help me to shake this selfish desire and to be a light of love, hope, and warmth to my patients today. AMEN.

For My Staff

My Father who art in heaven, my staff is really unhappy and dissatisfied. I am their leader, so it is up to me to "fix" their problems. I feel so inadequate and hopeless. Some of their problems are personal; some are related to staffing shortages; some are due to the complexity of our patients. Give me wisdom to help my staff and patience to know that I cannot be successful all at once. Allow all of them to experience your love through me, so that together we can have a happy working environment. Help us all to focus on our patients and not on ourselves. AMEN.

For Understanding in a Disaster

My God, what could make another human being harm others? As we work diligently to help all of these traumatized people, give us direction and endurance. As we treat the injured, allow us to be a source of comfort in this disaster to our patients and their families. AMEN.

For Making a Career Decision

Dear Father, my guide, I have worked as a nurse for almost thirty years. I am contemplating resigning my position. I feel the need to simplify my life and to give more of my time and attention to my spouse. Help me to make the right decision, for I know that my years of experience are valuable to others. Lord, I want to decide according to your will for my life. Guide my decision. AMEN.

For Working with the Dying

My God, the beginning and the end,
you give us life. You give us opportunities
to make a difference in the lives of others.
Help us to make a difference in how life
ends. AMEN.

Starting an I. V.

God of beginnings, as I start this I. V.,
assist me in being gentle and encouraging
to this patient entrusted to my care. Use
the flow of fluids and medicines into her
lifeblood to help in the healing we so
desire. Enable my eyes and hands to be
attentive to the flow in the I. V. and to the
patient, who also waits and watches.
AMEN.

For Healing from Medications

O great Provider, These medications are resources from nature and laboratory. Use them to heal and sustain, comfort and nourish, mend and make new, even bring destruction so that renewed health may come forth. AMEN.

Waiting for the Ambulance

O Shelter from the Stormy Blast, our team waits. We wait for the arrival of the ambulance. We both know and don't know what we are facing. Our training has prepared us to respond; but each patient is different and unique, not only with an injury or illness but also with a name. As we provide our skills, remind us that there is a person in the midst of our quickened, lifesaving work. AMEN.

For Guidance

Our God, the Morning Star, enlighten my path to work today. You have led me this far in the ministry of healing. Help me to anticipate your guidance today as I offer hope to those in need. Give me hope, too! AMEN.

For the Ending of the Day

O Alpha and Omega, the day is done;
but all are not yet well. Remind me,
though, God Who is Able, that in spite of
what I have seen and will see again and
again, "all will indeed be well; every
manner of thing will be well."* May I
return to work tomorrow encouraged not
by what I can do, but by what you will do
in your time. AMEN.

*Julian of Norwich

On Fixing Lunch

O Bread of Life, bless this food I will take to work today. I don't know when I will have time to eat, but please know that I am grateful to be able to take nourishment for my body whenever I can. May I take for myself that I may be strengthened to give to others. AMEN.

For Physicians

O Giver of life eternal, bless the
physicians with whom we work. Use our
respective skills and experiences to help us
achieve our common goals. Unite us in our
calling to care with compassion. Thank
you for the physicians who have great
knowledge and even greater wisdom.
AMEN.

For the Health Team

O Source of all healing, there are many on this health team. They have their tasks and I have mine. I pray that we will continually strive to work hard, to share the load, to adapt, to be creative, to forgive, and to forget. I pray for the nutritionist, the social worker, the pharmacist, the therapists, and the clerical staff. Lord, there are others; I name them before you now: Help us all. AMEN.

Before a Staff Meeting

O God of community, in this staff meeting keep us focused on our patients. Help us strive to hear before we speak and to resolve our conflicts fairly. Temper our convictions with wisdom. AMEN.

My Role in a Staff Meeting

Dear God, there are so many details and personalities to deal with in these meetings. Help me to contribute, but not to dominate. Help me to see and hear what others are trying to show and speak. Remind me: Team and Community; Patient First. AMEN.

On Changing Shifts

O God, our strength, who grants rest and peace, I have changed shifts from days to nights. The change is great and my adjustment is slow. Bear with me and bear me up, for "the spirit indeed is willing, but the flesh is weak."* Encourage me so that I might endure and come through this time of transition. AMEN.

*Matthew 26:41

When Charting

O Giver of wisdom, I must chart what I
have observed and how I have provided
nursing knowledge and skill to these
patients. Guide my remembering and
recounting of events so that I will be
accurate in my documentation, to show
that care is always present in the details.
Remind me of my commitment to
excellence. AMEN.

For a Patient Going to Surgery

O God who does not forsake us, my patient goes to surgery soon; and we both know there is no such thing as "minor surgery." To go under anesthesia is to enter into the unknown and to be at the will of the surgeon and team. Surround my patient with your steadfast love that helps us rest in you wherever we are, wherever we go. May the events of this day further the healing in this life you have entrusted to our care. AMEN.

For Those Who Wait

O waiting Father, I thank you that,
called upon or not, you are present in the
midst of our trials. Be present with the
family who anxiously awaits a blessing as
the surgery concludes and the surgeon
announces the outcome. You are the one
who waits with open arms for us to seek
you. Greet all of us wanderers, for we are
all in need of your unmerited favor, your
amazing grace. AMEN.

Before Performing a Painful Procedure

O God who hurts with us, this procedure will hurt my patient and test her endurance. Strengthen me during her groaning and cries as I too feel the burden of the pain. Match my compassion to my skill. May this painful effort to help be swift and accurate so that the ordeal is brief. AMEN.

For a Severely Depressed Patient

O God of your servant Job, I have a
patient who is severely depressed after
going through so much in such a short
period of time. How long, O Lord? We
treat with medications and words and
time. I also pray and wait and even sit at
the bedside without speaking. Remind me
of the power of silent presence. Help me to
make the time to be present with this
sufferer even "with sighs too deep for
words."* Praise be to God. AMEN.

*Romans 8:26

For a Demanding Patient

O God of infinite understanding, I have a difficult, demanding patient whose needs seem to know no bounds! Whatever I offer is taken, and then more is requested in no uncertain terms! Lord, I may never understand the depths of this patient's fears. Help me to "not rely on [my] own insight" but "in all [my] ways acknowledge [you]."* Help us to seek together the One who can answer our greatest needs. AMEN.

*Proverbs 3:5b, 6a

At a Birth

O God of new beginnings, I have been present at the birth of new life. I rejoice in your ongoing gift of life and delight in your unceasing creation. How wonderful is the arrival of babies; it is a way to let us know that your world should go on and have a future. Thank you for the opportunity to enter into the joy of this new family of parents and child. Birth is still a marvel in a world too often rendered dull by our failure to see that "in Christ . . . everything has become new!"* Amen.

*2 Corinthians 5:17

For Bearing Witness

Eternal Word, I humbly ask that you would help me to integrate my knowledge of your Word with my words to my patients. I instruct, I describe, I ask, I comfort with words, all to provide healing and care to the sick. Guide me in bearing witness to the Living Word when I am with my patients. Let my witness speak through my skills and care, but also help me to be sensitive when opportunities to speak of you are offered. Make me "be as wise as serpents and innocent as doves"* when speaking about concerns of faith. Remind me that as I enter a patient's room, I enter into holy ground! Amen.

*Matthew 10:16

Laughter

O God of Abraham and Sarah, remind me that laughter is healthy and that there are times when it is better to laugh than to cry. There are times when laughter is the only response to the fatigue of the day, the only response to the absurdities of modern health care, the only response to our human failings with our colleagues. Let my laughter be appropriate to my calling so that I never appear insensitive to those who hurt. May my humor lift up and not tear down. May laughing be a way of entering into the lives of others as we all anticipate the joy of the kingdom of God now and forever. AMEN.

A Prayer During Quiet Time in the Chapel

O Lord God, who once spoke in a still, small voice to Elijah, speak to me now in the silence of this sanctuary. Outside this room is the intensity of words and thoughts, knowledge and study, all for the benefit of the people hospitalized here. Lord, it is the work of nursing, but I also need the "work" of prayer in solitude. Thank you for this quiet place for my soul. AMEN.

Prayer on the Way to Work

Morning has broken, O Lord, and I start anew to be the kind of nurse you would have me be. Let me serve with skill and compassion, with courage and strength, with humility and yet with the boldness to do your will. Help me to see your will as we work together today. AMEN.

At the End of a Shift

Dear Lord, here I am at the end of a long day. Did I do my best? I'm not so sure. Forgive me. I tried and now I am tired. Give me rest so that I can begin again tomorrow. Help make it all new and fresh once again. Let there be no nameless patients ever for me! AMEN.

For the Physician

O Great Physician, bless your earthly
physicians who strive for healing through
the arts and sciences. Their training is
arduous, their knowledge is great. We ask
much of them. May I work with them as
an equal on tasks that are ours to share.
Remind us that we are all human and
limited, but we can do great things for
others when we do it together, shoulder to
shoulder. Give us strength for the long
days as we seek restored health for others.
Help us to make a difference through your
power and through the gifts of faith, hope,
and love. AMEN.

As a "Stat/Code Blue" Begins

O Lord, Help me! Help the team! Be with the patient! Help now! Be here now!

Lord, skill and compassion; skill and compassion now!

Lord, here we go! Go with us. May there be healing; may there be healing! Amen!

Prayer Over Medications

O God of all healing properties, these medications will combine with this patient's individual mind, body, and spirit. They have the power to change the human physiology. Use this power for the good of the patient. Help these medications to bring the desired change for the better, relief from pain, and rest for the weary. AMEN.

Waiting for a New Patient

O God of all time and space, I wait not knowing this patient's name or family or faith. I do not know the past events that might have brought on this injury or illness. Lord, I greet the unknown with my training and my eagerness to save life and limb. I do this as part of a team. O God, be present on our team as we await the unknown. AMEN.

After a Misunderstanding

O God of perfect wisdom, I pray for
wisdom in answering the criticism of a
patient. I believe that I have been
misunderstood. This misunderstanding has
come between us, and we must begin again
to share a mutual trust. If I have failed in
my care, please forgive me; if I have been
wronged, may I be swift to forgive. Be our
Mediator so that healing may come to this
relationship and help it begin anew. AMEN.

Witnessing to One of Another Faith

O Lord, in whom there is no East or West, my patient is not of my faith. In my witness may I be wise and recognize "a time to keep silence, and a time to speak."* May I show forth your love in the cheerful care I give, and may this be acceptable in your sight. Whatever my witness, may it be in the power of the Holy Spirit. AMEN.

*Ecclesiastes 3:7b

For a Patient Who Has Received Bad News

O Lord of good news, I soon will be with a patient who has received bad news. The diagnostic tests reveal a serious illness with limited successful treatments. Our hearts will be heavy together. Show me ways to be there for emotional support and grant me courage in showing that support. When I return home today, help me to take nothing for granted but to "give thanks in all circumstances."* Amen.

*1 Thessalonians 5:18

To Serve in Your Name

O Immanuel, in my work today with patients and families, I have observed the church serving. I give you thanks for sending us forth to serve in your name. Quietly, skillfully, compassionately, I see the gift of love offered in so many ways. Truly your body has hands and feet, eyes and ears to offer you to the world. Some will never know their care is done in your name. To you, the very source of that care, we offer our praise and thanksgiving. AMEN.

A Prayer for a New Employee

Gracious God of new beginnings, I pray for the new employee who joins our staff today. Where there is anxiety about this new beginning, help me to bring a warm welcome, a helping hand, a guiding voice. Let my supervision show forth our high standards, demonstrated in a gentle manner and with the intent that we will be team players. I pray this for the sake of those in our care. AMEN.

For the Lonely

O God of the still, small, voice, I pray for those in the depths of loneliness. Some are without family and some have family who do not visit or call. They have the unrelenting burden of feeling abandoned. The days here are like years. And even some who have families have such a history of conflict that they too feel isolated and without emotional support. Grant me wisdom in entering their saddened, shadowy world of illness. Help me to bear witness in word and deed to our mutual kinship in the One who made us all brothers and sisters in the Body of Christ. AMEN.

For One Whose Life Is Forever Changed

O One who is able to keep us all from falling, today I see one of my long-term patients leave for the rehabilitation center. There are permanent injuries that have led to a physically challenged life. A life has changed forever. A family will never be the same again. I pray for your strength to accompany them through the shadowy valleys they will pass. My patient will never ascend into the mountains as once before, but my faith says you will help this family see what promises yet await them on your horizon. Lord, help us to look for you no matter where we find ourselves. AMEN.

To Bring Comfort

Crucified and resurrected Lord, send your Holy Spirit, the Comforter, to go with me. I must soon tell my patient of a death in her family, even as she is now recovering from a serious illness. I have the words I must say, but I need your gentle guidance in bringing bad news. I need encouragement that your good news will also find a way into her life, into her grief. With you all things are possible. Each birth, each death is in the day that you have made. Help us to rejoice and be glad in that day. Walk down this hallway with me, O God, and "let the words of my mouth and the meditation of my heart be acceptable in your sight."* Amen.

*Psalm 19:14a

Let Me Rest in You

O God, as I sit in our hospital chapel, I thank you for the silence, for the retreat from the sounds of suffering and from the clatter of our medical technology. I welcome the touch of your eternity in this solitude before I return to the constant round of nursing skills, attentiveness, and tasks. Let me rest in you for this moment. AMEN.

For Your Constant Love and Care

O God of unending mystery, God of
infinite love, I echo the prayers of many of
my patients and their families: not so
much "Why me?" but "Why now?" The
expected future, the planned life, the sense
of safety can all be taken away so quickly. I
acknowledge that life is fragile. I seek to
handle it with care. But I do cry out with
my patients, "My God, my God, why . . . ?"
I pray for wisdom in remembering we are
the creation, not the Creator. Yet also
remind us, as you will, that you created us
out of love and for love, out of eternity and
for eternity. With this blessing we can
continue in spite of it all. Amen.